Streets of Character
A STROLL THROUGH THE STREETS OF
West Haddon

An illustrated history

First published 2002 by
West Haddon Local History Group
For information about the group, please
Contact the Hon. Secretary,
Sherry Calvert at
Ashleigh House, Crown Lane,
West Haddon,
Northants NN6 7AL

The publishers have made every effort to trace the copyright Owners of the photographs contained in this publication. Unless Otherwise stated, it is believed that these photographs are free of Copyright and within the public domain. If copyright has inadvertently been contravened, please inform the publishers in order that any error or omission may be corrected in future editions.

Copyright © 2002 by West Haddon Local History Group. All rights reserved. This book may not be reproduced, in whole or in part, in any form or by electronic or mechanical means, including information storage or retrieval systems, without the permission in writing from the copyright owners.

A CIP record is available from the British Library

Compiled by: Sherry Calvert
Designed by: Brian and Helen Allen
Edited by: Michael Clarke
Typeset in Times New Roman
Printed on: 115 gsm Chromomat (text), 280 gsm Chromomat (cover)
Printed by: Bullivant & Son, York. Tel: 01904 623241

Front Cover: Station Road from the Church Tower 1997.

Contents.

1	ACKNOWLEDGEMENTS	1
2	INTRODUCTION	2
3	Station Road	4
4	High Street	14
5	Northampton Road	30
6	Guilsborough Road	32
7	Morrison Park Road, Muncaster Way, Lattimore, Parnell and Worcester Closes	38
8	Atterbury Close, Field Close and Dairy Close	42
9	Old Forge Drive	44
10	West End	46
11	Outlying Properties	51
12	Appendix	53

Acknowledgments.

It would not have been possible to write this book without the sterling work done by John and Wendy Raybould and other members of West Haddon Local History Group in the past. Their research was the basis from which I started in 1995. John Raybould's death in the summer of 2000 made me realise that I needed to get on with my research if I was ever going to get this work published.

The current members of the group have been most supportive and this is their book. I am merely the mouthpiece.

I am most grateful to Michael Clarke who edited this book and to Colin Adams who corrected some glaring errors. I also talked to many people most of whom have lived in and around West Haddon for all of their lives. These include Sid Adams, Cecil Ainge, Edna Broadhurst, Mary Bush, Michael Bush, Ken Croxford, Jacky Dawson, Anne Drewitt, Sidney Garrett, Freda Hopper, Madeleine, Philip and Elaine Litchfield, Greta Orcherton, Kathleen Overton, Hilda Stanley, Daniel Stratford, Keith Taylor and Gill Warne.

This is no way meant to be a definitive history of the village, merely the recording of some aspects of the streets, houses and people, which may otherwise be lost.

Sherry Calvert 2002

Introduction.

West Haddon, a village mentioned in the Domesday Book, stands at an extended crossroads where the old turnpike road from Dunchurch to Northampton, now the A428, meets the road from Market Harborough to Daventry and Banbury. A milestone, defaced in the Second World War, stands outside the Old Post House at number 34, High Street. It once gave the distances to Northampton and to Dunchurch, which were the nearest staging posts on the turnpike now the A428, and to London.

Until the late 18th century, 'roads' were grassy tracks which gave access to the strips of cultivated land in the fields.

Under the Parliamentary Enclosure Act for the village in 1765, not only were the field sizes and owners laid down but also the major roads. It was specified that the new owners of each field were to make sure that any of these roads crossing their land were 40 feet wide. The turnpike road was to be 60 feet wide. All these roads were named, mainly according to their destination e.g. Yelvertoft Road, Crick Road.

Many houses were and still are known locally by the names of the residents or the use to which they were put.

This booklet attempts to explain some of these road names and house names. They all have a story to tell.

In 1964 West Haddon Parish Council took a momentous decision to organise the official numbering of the houses in the village, to create a harmonious integrated scheme. Prior to that, houses seem to have had piecemeal addresses, or were simply known by their owner's name. It took some time to put the scheme in to action. The last house on Guilsborough Road had the address 16 Guilsborough Road in 1968/69. By the following year it had become 76 Guilsborough Road, as the rent books on the following page show. The scheme which the Council put in place has remained basically the same but greatly added to over the years.

Of the names of the current through roads in the village most are self-explanatory, but the fourth major road, leading towards Daventry is Station Road until it leaves the village when it becomes Watford Road.

DAVENTRY RURAL DISTRICT COUNCIL

RENT CARD — 1968-69   B

Medical Officer of Health: Dr. J. M. St. V. DAWKINS, M.B.B.S., D.P.H., D.C.H.
R.D.C. Offices, Church Walk, Daventry

Landlord or Agent: DAVENTRY RURAL DISTRICT COUNCIL
TEL.: DAVENTRY 2184/5

Standard Weekly Rent .... £ 1 : 18 : 5

Commencement of Tenancy ....
(If after 1st April 1968)

MR. D. STRATFORD,
16, GUILSBORO ROAD,
WEST HADDON. RUGBY.

16/30

IMPORTANT — It is most essential that this card be produced when a payment is made

Summary of Secs. 77, 78 & 80 of the Housing Act, 1957
1. An occupier who causes or permits his dwelling to be overcrowded is liable to prosecution for an offence under the Housing Act, 1957, and, if convicted, to a fine of not exceeding five pounds. Any part of a house which is occupied by a separate family is a "dwelling".
2. A dwelling is overcrowded if the number of persons sleeping in it is more than the "permitted number", or is such that two or more of those persons, being ten years old or over, of opposite sexes (not being persons living together as husband and wife), must sleep in the same room.
3. The "permitted number" for the dwelling to which this Payment Card relates is .... persons. In counting the number of persons each child under ten years of age counts as half a person, and a child of less than one year is not counted at all.
4. The Act contains special provisions relating to overcrowding already existing or which is due to a child attaining the age of either one or ten years, or which is due to exceptional circumstances. Full information about these special provisions and all provisions as to overcrowding can be obtained free on application to the Local Authority whose address is printed on this card.
8

THIS CARD IS THE PROPERTY OF THE COUNCIL

2604367   Alfred Gilbert & Sons, Ltd., London, N.W.9   1974

DAVENTRY RURAL DISTRICT COUNCIL

RENT CARD — 1971-72   B

Medical Officer of Health: Dr. J. M. St. V. DAWKINS, M.B.B.S., D.P.H., D.C.H.
R.D.C. Offices, Church Walk, Daventry

Landlord or Agent: DAVENTRY RURAL DISTRICT COUNCIL
Telephone: DAVENTRY 2184/5

Standard Weekly Rent .... £1·92

Commencement of Tenancy ....
(if after 1st April 1971)

MR. D. STRATFORD,
76, GUILSBORO ROAD,
WEST HADDON. RUGBY.

76/30

IMPORTANT — It is most essential that this card be produced when a payment is made.

Summary of Secs. 77, 78 & 80 of the Housing Act, 1957
1. An occupier who causes or permits his dwelling to be overcrowded is liable to prosecution for an offence under the Housing Act, 1957, and, if convicted, to a fine not exceeding five pounds. Any part of a house which is occupied by a separate family is a "dwelling".
2. A dwelling is overcrowded if the number of persons sleeping in it is more than the "permitted number", or is such that two or more of those persons, being ten years old or over, of opposite sexes (not being persons living together as husband and wife), must sleep in the same room.
3. The "permitted number" for the dwelling to which this Payment Card relates is .... persons. In counting the number of persons each child under ten years of age counts as half a person, and a child of less than one year is not counted at all.
4. The Act contains special provisions relating to overcrowding already existing or which is due to a child attaining the age of either one or ten years, or which is due to exceptional circumstances. Full information about these special provisions and all provisions as to overcrowding can be obtained free on application to the Local Authority whose address is printed on this card.
8—

THIS CARD IS THE PROPERTY OF THE COUNCIL

6486370   Alfred Gilbert & Sons, Ltd., London, N.W.9   1794

Rent Books Showing Change of House Number.

Station Road.

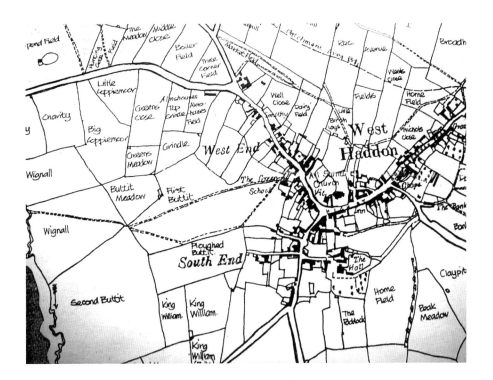

Field Survey.

The field survey map of 1932 compiled by pupils at the village school shows the area around Station Road, Hardays Lane and Staffords Lane as 'South End'. 'End' often occurs as a name for a 'new' extension to an old village and so this may have been an extension to the original village which clustered around the High Street.

Station Road may have been known as Spinney Lane at the time of the Parliamentary Enclosure Act in 1765. A spinney is a small group of trees so perhaps there were more trees than there are now. It may have referred to Crow Spinney on Watford Road, just past the Washbrook. The station referred to in the present name is Welton Station, located between Watford village and the A5 trunk road in Watford Parish. It shows how greatly the railways affected the surrounding area. The railway line was built between 1834 and 1838 as part of the North Western railway, by the Stephensons (father and son), and offered a complete range of passenger and freight services. The station was called Welton to avoid the risk of confusing Watford in Northamptonshire with the larger Watford Junction, near London. Photos in the Local History Group archive reveal that old signposts actually said 'To Welton Station'.

Signpost to Welton Station.

More than just a station, this small settlement, quite separate from Watford Village may have originated as a canal settlement (like nearby Buckby Wharf), and even in this new millennium, local people refer to Welton Station as a place rather than a facility.

There is a natural break in the Northamptonshire uplands here, Watford Gap, created by overflow channels during the Ice Age. The original flow of water towards the north was trapped by the advancing ice. A lake was created which eventually found an outlet towards the south east through the hills. The flowing water eroded a deep valley. This natural phenomenon has been used for communication links since the Romans first built Watling Street, along the route of the present day A5, to hasten their armies north to quell the unruly tribes. As the road and the canal funnelled into this gap, it was natural that the railway would follow the same line. But the arrival of the railway in the early 1800s marked a decline in the economy of West Haddon as goods were transferred by rail rather than the slower turnpike, and cattle were no longer driven to market on foot. The canal too went in to decline.

In turn the railway was eclipsed by the motorway built in 1959, still using the same gap. However today's villagers do still remember goods such as sugar beet still being transported from there during World War Two. After the War, cattle were also offloaded there and walked up to West Haddon for fattening.

The passenger station eventually closed on 7th July 1958, but goods trains continued to stop there for some time longer. The original goods yard and sheds can still be spotted from Watford Road, on the eastern side of the line, but in disrepair and likely to be demolished.

Because the station was such an important facility, the road leading to it from West Haddon was renamed Station Road. Trade directories in the early 20th century stated that West Haddon could be found three and one quarter miles North East of Welton Station.

There are several side roads, all cul-de-sacs, off Station Road. The first on the right as you leave the village is Staffords Lane. The Stafford family seem to have lived in the village in the 18th century, perhaps at a house along this lane. Other than the odd entries in the parish registers, virtually nothing has been discovered about them. A Victorian trade directory mentions the old workhouse in Staffords Lane. This was built, probably around 1755, and was not the fearsome institution of Dickensian tradition.

It would probably have been a refuge for unmarried mothers, the disabled or the old who found themselves unable to manage on their own. It is unlikely to have been more than just a cottage.

This lane was also known as Pudding Bag Lane, a delightfully quaint descriptive name which is found in other villages in the area. This was an early term for a cul-de-sac, named after a familiar household item. Number Three, Staffords Lane is Pudding Bag Cottage, keeping this name alive.

Pudding Bag Cottage.

The next side road on your right, leaving the village, is Harday's Lane, named after a medical man, Dr Harday. The actual spelling of his surname is generally Harday, but sometimes Hardy. These corruptions were common in an age where names were passed on by word of mouth. On the 1900 map of the village, this lane was called Buttit Lane, presumably because it led to the fields of Buttit Farm. Field names there include First and Second Buttit, and Buttit Meadow. 'Buttit' may be a corruption of the old field name Buttoft, 'toft' being the Norse word around this part of the country for a homestead, and reminding us that Northamptonshire was part of Danelaw, the Danish-controlled areas of the Midlands and Northern England in the 9th century. It was still known locally as Buttit Lane in the 1950s. Hardy's Cottage stands at the junction of the lane with Station Road, and Harday's House, a fine 19th century building, stands in the lane itself. This house appears on Bryant's 1827 map of the county, so it may have been modernised by Dr Harday who was active in the village from 1857, where for 35 years he continued to work at his profession. He was born in Northampton in 1821 and lived to be 83. His obituary, published on 30th September 1904, mourns the passing of one of West Haddon's most notable and respected inhabitants. He was identified with all the local charities, including the Heygate School, and was said almost "to have known the works of Dickens by heart", and was fond of quoting him and other scholars. Indeed "he rarely conversed long without quoting some pithy sentence". He and his wife Fanny are buried in the churchyard with their only daughter, who was just 25 when she died in 1896.

Harday's house then became the home of the Heygates, a large respected West Haddon family. This explains the name of the house next door, Heygates Barn, which has been extensively renovated. John Heygate Esq. is mentioned in a Kelly's Trade directory as having endowed the village school, large enough for 170 children, in 1837. John and William Heygate, presumably next generation, appear in the 1854 directory as grazier and farmer respectively. It was common practice to name the son after the father but can make identification very difficult. Their descendants still live in and around the village. When the vault under West Haddon church was opened in 1979, many tombs and references to the family were found dating from 1820 to 1850. We know that Leonard William Heygate married Evelyn Underwood in 1920, moving to Creaton and then back to the village and Harday's House. There are several farms named Heygate in the area around West Haddon.

Daisy and Mary Atterbury from another well known village family bought Harday's house before the Second World War. The building has certainly been added to over the years. If you visit the delightful gardens on Open Garden day in July, take time to look at the different building materials which have been used. The current owner commented that rooms seem to have been added on here and there on both storeys as demand for accommodation grew.

The longevity of family history in an area was thought unusual by the eminent historian W.G. Hoskins of Leicester University. He found in his studies of the county that, in general, family names petered out after three or four generations. Not in every village, Professor Hoskins!

At the end of Hardays Lane was a conker tree - a horse chestnut - much prized by village schoolboys. There were also three walnut trees which got raided. The walnut's outer covering leaves a yellow dye on your hands. Woe betide you if this incriminating evidence was found!

Symington's Corset factory also stood in Station Road, near Stafford's Lane, some way back from the road. Factory is perhaps a rather grand title for it: it was a large shed. Village girls were employed as outworkers, and it closed when Symington's opened another factory in Rugby. At number three Station Road, near the centre of the village, is Crystal House, thought to date from the mid 1600s. It probably got its name from the stunning number of glazed windows, particularly upstairs, which were a very visible sign of wealth in the 17th century. You got taxed on the number of windows you had!

We know that John Walker lived at Crystal House, as in 1750 he sold some barns which were part of his farm, including numbers five and seven Station Road. Number five is the Old Bake House, and by June 15th 1868 was owned by Matthias Horton. On that day, there was a disastrous fire which ruined the Hortons. Charred timbers have been found by the couple who are currently renovating the property. The Bake House opened again and was run by 'Fiddler' Cross, then the Coopers and then the Tyrells until the middle of the 20th century, baking Sunday roasts for families in its huge oven at the back of the house. Baking last took place there in 1957. Older villagers remember calling in to leave their roast dinner there to cook whilst going on to church or chapel, as until the mid 20th century, the Sabbath was strictly observed: children were forbidden to play in the streets, and it was generally a day of rest (but presumably not for the baker!).

Following the appearance of Crystal House on the television programme Gardeners' World in 1992, for the first Open Gardens Day in West Haddon, quite a lot has been found out about it. The house was recognised by Mrs. Roberts, the granddaughter of previous residents, Mr. and Mrs. James Adams. She corresponded at length with Mr. and Mrs. Hughes who lived there in 1992. She remembered a well and a pump in the garden and the adjacent barns being used as a carpenter's shop. Trees were brought in here to the sawpit for processing and one product was coffins. There was a diphtheria epidemic in the late 1920s and early 30s when a great number of small coffins were needed. When Mr. Adams died in

1934, Mrs. Adams moved in to one of the almshouses in Crick Road. Their daughter had married T.A. Roberts ('Ole Tom' of the *Northampton Mercury and Herald*) - against her family's wishes, for he was deemed impecunious. She wished to be married at the old Wesleyan chapel in Guilsborough Road, of which she was an energetic member, but it was not licensed for such ceremonies, and special arrangements had to be made. It was possibly the only time a wedding was conducted there. When the chapel closed, Mrs. Roberts had the organ sent to her in London.

Crystal House.

The house fell in to disrepair. It was bought in 1936 for £100 by Sgt. Lord, a member of the local police force. "From the kitchen you could look straight up and out through a hole in the roof, where ivy was growing." The barns were used by the Home Guard for drilling during World War Two.

Further down Station Road, opposite Hardays Lane, is a short lane, 'the tradesmens entrance', leading to West Haddon Hall. Although one building, The Elms, does front on to this little lane, modern road naming practise has decreed that this property should have the address 29 Station Road and the little lane have no identity of its own. Dr Darley lived at 'Pear Trees', currently a guest house, on the corner, and kept his surgery just round the corner next to 29 in the late 1800's, early 1900's. He is shown in the 1891 census, aged 26, as a registered general practitioner: "neither employer nor employed".

There was no such thing as a waiting room or an appointments system. You just stood outside and waited to be seen. If it was raining, too bad! Remember too, that these services were charged for. You only went there if it was absolutely necessary. There are stories in the village that the good doctor sometimes used to let patients make up their own prescriptions so that he could get out onto the golf course!

West Haddon Hall and its grounds occupy a site to the left of Station Road, and was started in 1827 for William Judkins Dunkley, who was doing well as a grazier. Unfortunately he over speculated and by 1831 he was bankrupt. *Kelly's trade directory* of 1871 says it was owned by Thomas Smith Esq. followed by Owen C Wallis in 1898 and Claude Armitt Borritt in 1920. The Gage family owned it prior to World War II. There used to be several bungalows for servants in the grounds

During the War, the Hall was used for military purposes. The servicemen quartered there were "a godsend for extras during rationing". Towards the end of the war it was taken over for a short time to house evacuated children. Villagers remember nurses from Surrey working there.

When Lord Pritchard bought the Hall shortly after the war the top storey had already been removed by a Rugby firm who were able to leave the chimney stacks in place when lowering the roof. This brought the number of bedrooms down by 16 making it a more manageable size.

Further south, just down the hill on Station Road, is a 1960s development of houses, known as The Paddocks: when these houses were being built, Lord Pritchard paid for the ground to be excavated so that the houses fitted snugly into the hillside. Lady Pritchard is still the owner of the Hall today.

Laud's Cottage is by the entrance to the Hall. There is also a Laud's Road in Crick. Could this have anything to do with the Laud who was the inflammatory Archbishop of Canterbury, 1633-45, under Charles I ? Under, is it a play on words? It was once owned by Sgt Lord. The name Laud's cottage was given by the Barby family who knocked the four original cottages into one dwelling. They are shown on the Electoral register from 1980.

The back road to Long Buckby, once a gated road, branches off from Station Road just south of The Paddocks. Foxhill Road leads to an area of the parish known simply as Foxhill, and to Foxhill Manor. Built as a hunting lodge, and in existence by the 1880s, this is now an old people's home. Foxes are common around the village, and this is reflected in the topography of the parish - the area between West Haddon and Crick is known as Foxholes. Foxhill Manor was once the country seat of the Fitzroy family, and in 1920 home of Captain the Honourable Edward Algernon Fitzroy M.P., J.P., Speaker of the House of Commons. The magnificent range of stabling was frequently occupied by the horses of King George V during the hunting season.

Foxhill Manor.

The entire Fitzroy family were accustomed to walk to church every Sunday, rain or shine, and all the village children were required to curtsey or touch their caps as they passed.

Later the Wykeham family lived at Foxhill. Colonel Wykeham's wife Mildred was a member of the nursing committee which appointed Nurse Muncaster as District Nurse for the area. Mrs. Wykeham kept a jersey herd for milking, the milk being distributed to villagers by being poured from large churns into buckets before being ladled into people's jugs placed on their doorsteps. It was also sent to the major dairies in the churns. Harry Farn and Len Clarke also had milk rounds. Milk was an important agricultural product in this part of Northamptonshire, and the Local History Group has much detail in its archives on the production, storage and distribution of milk through the years.

High Street.

Most villages have a 'main street' which provides the focus for trade and commercial activity, as well as often the social and spiritual life of the community. It is also the point of contact with passing traffic, particularly in a village like West Haddon that grew up with, and was dependent on, trade from travellers on the route between Northampton and Rugby. West Haddon's High Street is the location of two of the current licensed premises and one of its oldest buildings as well as its parish church, with its memorial to the dead of two world wars.

**War Memorial in Original Position
With the Lee Children.**

The War Memorial, dedicated in 1920, once stood at the junction of Station Road, High Street and West End. Originally wooden, the money to fund it was raised by public subscription. Captain Fitzroy from Foxhill started the fund with a donation of 5 and a half guineas (£5.77 today but worth a great deal more then). It was replaced in stone and became the meeting place for children of the village who sat and climbed on it. These were the days before road traffic presented any threat - traffic was so light in the village, that even just after the Second World War, older villagers remember playing spinning tops in the street outside.

Children used to be marched up to the memorial from the village school on Remembrance Day, 11th November, each year, to pay tribute to those who had fallen in both World Wars. As time went by, the ceremony was moved to the nearest Sunday. Villagers also remember assembling there on Ascension Day. A growing volume of traffic on the main road through the village and damage to the Memorial meant it had to be moved into the grounds of All Saints Church in the early 1960s, where it still stands. This improved the flow of traffic through the village. By 1992, matters had come full circle and it was decided that the traffic was travelling too fast through the village, making it hazardous for anyone, but in particular children and the elderly, to cross the road. Heavy lorries in particular were a problem. Pedestrians were being 'sucked' off the footpath and the spray thrown up by the traffic was eroding the soft sandstone foundations of walls and houses. A 'traffic calming' scheme was introduced, with a 'mini roundabout' being installed where once the Memorial stood. A second roundabout was constructed at the other end of the High Street, with 'gateways' on all the major roads into the village, and a shuttle in Guilsborough Road which only allows traffic through in one direction at a time. West Haddon, along with the other Northamptonshire villages of Crick and Byfield, was the first to test this method of traffic control. Even this has failed to tackle the root cause of the problem - the sheer volume of motor traffic using the road. A survey in 2000, connected with possible plans for a bypass, long demanded by villagers, estimated daily volumes at more than 6,000 vehicles passing through the High Street.

The first mini roundabout is probably roughly where the turnpike gates used to be. There was a booth which controlled three gates, closing off all the roads. The Rugby (Dunchurch) to Northampton Road was a turnpike from about 1740, with a tollgate at Silsworth Lane, probably where Foxholes Garage is now. A further Act of Parliament in 1764 said that this tollgate should be removed and a new one erected in West Haddon, "near the Elm tree". A tollhouse was built nearby. We can only guess exactly where. The Commissioners were strictly told not to award a road "on the backside of the Town of West Haddon" - in other words a bypass!

Trade is the lifeblood of a community and the Turnpike was vital to the village economy of the day. It was obviously well used, as it is recorded that in 1784, £142 7s 3d was raised, twice as much as that at Hillmorton Gate in Rugby. The revenue raised was used to improve the awful state of the road. All villagers were supposed to give up some time each year to repair it.

There was also danger from footpads (highway thieves). In 1721 a Northampton cloth dealer took his wares to sell at Coventry Market. He was robbed of his takings on the road between Crick and West Haddon - some £21, a small fortune in those days!

The High Street has boasted one of the village's pubs for over 200 years: The Crown has always been of great importance to the village. There was much competition between it and the Red Lion (no longer a pub) which was in West End, for trade. Its position adjacent to the church is not unusual. As villages became established they clustered around their public buildings - the pub and the church. Was the village on King Charles I's side in the English Civil War? The Civil War Battle of Naseby took place in 1645, a few miles from the village, so perhaps the pub was declaring its allegiance. The sign of the Crown has been interpreted in various ways over time, but remains an easily recognised symbol. It has changed hands and breweries many times. Phipps was the first large brewery to own it, buying it in 1879.

The Crown was the site of the great West Haddon riot. This was connected with the enclosure of common land in the village which was a very disputed issue. Richard and Nathaniel Parnell (Parnells Close off Guilsborough Road is named after the family) are on record as having opposed the Enclosure Act, 1765. There were a further 30 proprietors who did not give their consent. Some agreed that it might be beneficial in the long run but many of them could not afford the cost of fencing for the fields, some were too old and some simply couldn't be bothered. However, their whole way of life under the 'Open Field System' was about to change. The common land and heath disappeared.

After the second reading of the bill in the House of Commons, commissioners were appointed and matters appeared to go ahead smoothly. Then, on 29th July 1765, an advertisement appeared in the Northampton *Mercury* for 'Football Play' in West Haddon. This was a secret message to meet and cause trouble. A great number of people turned up, which became a tumultuous mob, pulling up and burning the fences of the new fields. Dragoons marched over from Northampton to restore order, but not before much damage was done. But enclosure went ahead anyway! West Haddon was the only Parish in Northamptonshire which put up serious opposition to the Act. The Parnells are not listed as being brought to trial after the riot so it must be assumed that they finally withdrew their opposition. No one ever discovered who put the advertisement in the paper.

The Crown.

The Crown was also involved in the notorious West Haddon murder, although the offence actually occurred in Crick in the late 1800s. A Mrs. Bates was charged with the murder of an old lady, Mrs. Gulliver, after she had been buried in our graveyard, and The Crown was the most handy place for the trial. The suspect took strychnine at the opening of the proceedings, and died within a few minutes. This caused great excitement and an inquest was held at "the inn which adjoined the churchyard". The whole thing was conducted at night for privacy and the dead bodies were brought in to the inn and removed again through the window of the club room.

The other current hostelry in the High Street, the Pytchley Hotel, was named after the famous local hunt. As we have seen at Foxhill, there were several hunting lodges in the area. The county generally was known for foxhunting in the late 1800s. The railway "allowed gentlemen to travel from London out to their hunting lodges which were numerous around here". So runs a local report. But there was controversy even then. The horses and riders destroyed the crops in their pursuit of their prey.

The Pytchley.

The Pytchley has only 'recently' become a hotel: in 1898, known as Westfield House, it was the private residence of William Darker. Mrs. Paul owned the house before the First World War, and she was involved in setting up the Women's Institute in the village. Four weary women who had finished a hard day's work making hay were seen by Mrs. Paul and invited for a cup of tea. She told them about an organisation which had started in Canada for the self-education of women from all walks of life. They obviously all thought the idea had merit as the West Haddon Women's Institute came into being on 18th March 1918.

Westfield House was then purchased by Mrs Proudfoot, who talked about making it in to a hotel, and Colonel Welman also lived there before the Second World War. The Ellis family owned it as Westfield hotel after the Second World War. There are early photographs of Westfield House without the distinctive semi-circular extensions which were added by Mr Jim Demetri the current owner.

The Parish Church of All Saints, West Haddon, stands on an elevated site to the south west of The Crown. A Norman church with substantial medieval parts, the fabric of the building has been altered over the years and a critical eye can detect evidence of this. It once had a wooden spire atop the tower, which was demolished in 1648. Perhaps the Parish was too poor to be able to afford to repair it or perhaps there was a severe shortage of wood after the Civil War. Photos of the church show that before the Second World War there were iron railings on top of the perimeter wall on High Street, which were taken away to help with the war effort. However one or two bars remain nestling in the hedge at the end of the wall nearest West End.

At the entrance to the steps leading to the church is a magnificent gateway of local sandstone with ironwork arch and gates. A plaque on the side announces that the arch is in memory of Dr Morrison, "born in 1902 and died in 1973 - well loved by his many friends". Morrison Park Road is named after him.

Churches are vital sources of evidence for the history of villages and their development, and All Saints is no exception. The Church played a crucial role in the secular, as well as the sacred, life of a village: for example, the church bell used to be rung daily by hand at noon and eight o'clock in the evening, for curfew. Agricultural workers in the fields near by could hear this. The churchyard to the rear remains a haven of peace surrounded by several mature trees. The whole is carefully tended by Sid Adams and Diana Butcher and has either won the 'Best Kept Churchyard' or been runner up many times. Closer inspection of the stones reveal much of the history of families in the village, with areas for the Atterburys and Heygates amongst others. Some of the gravestones at the front of the church were repositioned to make space for the War Memorial when it was moved to its current location. More about the Church can be found in *Milestones and memories*, and other Local History Group publications.

Opposite the church in the High Street is an imposing stone building, now two homes, Church House and Rye House. The whole building was once Church Farm and *might* have been where Daventry Priory set up its manager to collect tithes, the Priory owning the land in the Middle Ages. A tithe was one tenth of your income. We know that the tithe yard was on the opposite corner at the junction of

All Saints Church Gates and inset showing Plaque.

West End and Station Road and much of the tithe payment would have been in produce. It was the family home of Marcia Field, later Marcia Williams, Lady Faulkender, close confidante of Labour Prime Minister Harold Wilson, in the 1960s and 70s. Her father, Harry Field, was the manager of the brick works in Long Buckby, and built the newer house next door, whilst living at Church Farm. This newer house was then owned by Mr Lattimore, headmaster of West Haddon Primary School, after whom Lattimore Close, a new development off Morrison Park Road is named.

On the same side of the road, number eight, is an interesting building which has been a shop for more than a century - it is currently (2001) a collectibles shop. Until 1995, it was Matilda's Dress Shop. In 1865, it opened as a daughter shop of the wealthy Long Buckby Co-op, and was known as the West Haddon Investment and Provident Self Assistance Society. Managers over the years were Mr. Robbins, Mr. Letts, and then Freddie Spring, who was a native of Ravensthorpe.

Number 8 High Street.

The store sustained serious fire damage in 1891 after someone accidentally knocked over an oil lamp. Restoration resulted in the building being carefully reduced in size with a column and pediment being moved nearer to the front door. Several windows and doors have been blocked up. There was an oil lamp outside, with the site of the bracket from which it hung still visible. One older villager, still alive, was a lamp lighter when he was about twelve years old. There was also a lamp on Slyes Green at the western entrance to the village, and one on the Green in West End.

Mr. and Mrs. Freddie Spring lived in a thatched cottage that used to stand between number eight and the Victorian house, number 12. This plot was turned into a garden when the cottage was demolished after Mrs. Spring died. A domestic garage, part of Barber's Antiques, was built there in 1999. The retaining wall built at the end of Barber's Antiques collapsed in a spectacular fashion after some very cold weather on New Year's Day 2001, revealing details of the once larger house.

Middlesex Cottage at number 24 was designed and built for two nurses, the Misses Cross, by George Townley, assisted by Jo Adams the undertaker. These sisters trained at the Middlesex Hospital in London and were both honoured during the First World War, according to a report in the *Mercury and Herald* for 1915. The senior Miss Cross was awarded the French Government Medal of Honour, one of only two English women so honoured at the time, for combating epidemics. Contracting diphtheria on a hospital ship at Dunkirk she came back to recuperate at her brother's house in West Haddon. Her sister, Miss Sarah Cross, nursed 200 people following the Kingston, Jamaica, earthquake of 1907. On their retirement, plans and sketches of the house were drawn and work started. It was only at this stage that it was realised that there was no staircase! One had hurriedly to be incorporated into the design. When they retired each of three doctors gave them a chair which took pride of place in the cottage. They must have been devoted, for they passed away within a short time of each other and are thought to have been buried in the churchyard with a headstone saying 'and in death they were not divided'. It has not so far been able to trace this. However there is a plaque with a dedication from Miss Cross on one of the pillars in church.

At number 34, is the Old Post House, adjacent to the current Post Office. At one time it had a bow window but extra tax was payable on that so it was removed. Jack Scarth lived there during the 1930s. He worked at the cutting edge of technology at Rugby Radio Station and had a wireless which picked up short wave broadcasts from overseas. Villagers packed in to hear reports from the USA about the latest Joe Louis fight. His son enrolled in the Royal Signals Corp in the Second World War and was one of the casualties.

On the opposite side of the road adjacent to the church, stands Brownstones, which was previously the Vicarage, before the current one was built in West End when the Reverend Porteous was in office. This is a descriptive name for a substantial house built of the local distinctive sandstone blocks. Sandstone was extracted for local building use from quarries at Winwick Warren and Harlestone, and the stone may have come from one of these. The original house was built by order of Thomas Wolsey just before his fall from favour with Henry VIII, concerning the King's desire to divorce Katherine of Aragon and marry Anne Boleyn. Wolsey died in disgrace 1530. The present house appears to date from 17th century - Pevsner dates it at 1676 - with Victorian additions. There are remains in the cellar of a blocked up window with stone work typical of the 16th century.

The Reverend Fauquier lived here as incumbent for All Saints, from 1850 until 1887. In a fascinating report which he left behind, he comments on how cold it was here compared to Norfolk, how things weren't what they used to be - cricket outfits for one thing - and how he was not received into County society as he thought befitted his station in life. The purchase of his advowson (the right to be the vicar) for £4655, he thought, was "an unfortunate and imprudent Act", as it fell in value by his old age to about £3000. In addition, the cottagers, middle and lower classes, expected him to shake hands when he met them.

Rumour has it that there was once an underground passage from here to The Sheaf public house opposite.

Well Cottage, at number nine High Street, (and there is another Well Cottage in West End) shows us how important it was to get water. There is no surface stream in the village - the nearest streams form the parish boundary, with Guilsborough in the north east, and with Watford in the south west.

West Haddon stands on a spring line, where sandy pervious rock through which water can run sits on an impervious clay layer. As water can no longer percolate down into the ground, it is forced to the surface as a spring or can be tapped via a well. In Station Road, even in the very dry summer of 1995, water was constantly heard running under the grid near to the Foxhill Road junction. Old maps show many houses in the village having their own spring or other private water source, but there was also public provision. There used to be a long handled pump outside the cottages on the opposite side of the road, where the small factory building is now. When that fouled up, it was replaced on the other side of the road by a tap which was demolished when The Paddocks was built. There were also several other public pumps in the village.

One fairly derelict one can still be seen in Northampton Road. There were others: by Crown Lane, in front of what was Cross the Butchers, just opposite the Crown, and in Guilsborough Road next to the Baptist Chapel. Piped water was brought in to the village between the wars, but not all houses were originally connected to the sewage system until the 1950s. There was a post windmill for pumping water to the nursery, near where the water tower now stands in Northampton Road. This tower is vital for feeding water to our taps.

The river Nene rises as a spring on the parish boundary between West Haddon Watford parishes and flows to the Wash in the east. The river Avon also rises as a spring in a garden in nearby Naseby parish and flows through Stratford into the Bristol Channel.

Derelict Village Pump.

We sit on the watershed of England. Water falling during a cloud burst either ends up in the North Sea or the Irish Sea depending on which part of West Haddon it falls on.

Springs and wells were a vital source of fresh water in the past. Today we tend to view them as a nuisance. Water floods cellars and undermines walls. It creates a motoring hazard when, as in the summer of 1999, there was a torrential rainstorm and the drains were unable to cope, turning the High Street into a large stream. It was discovered that the old pipes and sewers had collapsed, forming a blockage under the road outside the Post Office. There had been problems in 1953 when mains sewerage was built in the village, with running sand encountered in West End.

The Flooded High Street - Summer 1999.

Manchester House, at 11 High Street, was repointed in the early 1990s. Rendering on the sign above the door, which had been a black oblong, was removed to reveal cast lettering which had previously only been vaguely discernible when the sun shone on it from a westerly direction. The legend 'Townley Tailor and Draper' was revealed. It is thought that this house was so named because it was a shop and had a warehouse of cotton ('Manchester') goods - the house name occurs in other villages. Its position on the Turnpike road would have made it a good distribution point for clothes and household items. Garments such as labourers' shirts were sent out ready to 'make' and local women were able to earn some money to stretch the housekeeping by making them up for the shop. Villagers remember the large awning outside, and the displays in the windows. In the left hand one were tins of dubbin, linament and snuff. Clothes were in the right hand window. Around the corner in Crown Lane were leggings, boots and men's clothing. A cobbler worked here at one time.

Not much is known about Verwood House across Crown Lane, except that it was built by Mr Luck from Long Buckby. Sid Incley lived there at one time, before he went to live on The Green. The owner of an impressive Buick car, he had three sons, one of whom, Ken, a boxer, had a formidable reputation in his time. When Mr. Crawley, the butcher, owned Avenue House, villagers remember boxing bouts being promoted there. Randolph Turpin was one of the star turns. He was born in 1928 and beat Sugar Ray Robinson in 1951, so at a guess, this was happening not long after the Second World War. One villager remembers standing at the gate selling pies for 3d each from a basket as customers poured in. There was also boxing at Long Buckby Co-op Hall around then.

The small U shaped lane which runs off High Street by the side of the Crown and joins it again between Manchester House and Verwood House is logically called Crown Lane. The recently opened Jurassic Way runs up by the Crown and turns left in front of Avenue House, continuing as an unsurfaced lane. This was known to lads in the village as 'Rec Lane' as it led to the recreation ground in a field at the northern end of the churchyard. Here was a sandpit, two swings, a wooden seesaw and two cross bars. There was also room to play games like pitch and toss. The playground moved to a field between Guilsborough Road and Northampton Road. The parish minutes record the fencing off of the allotments in April 1958.

The Jurassic Way crosses an open area in front of the Old Fire Station in Crown Lane. The area occupied by this and part of what is now the churchyard was once the village pound. Stray cattle and other animals were penned up by the pindar, an early sort of policeman, until their owners came to claim them. They had to pay a fine for letting them wander about in the first place. This was an important part of village organisation when, before 1765 and enclosure, the fields were open and unhedged and straying animals could do enormous damage among growing crops.

West Haddon had a three field system, South Field, West or Little Field and Dibdale or Deepdale. There was also an area of heath and waste out towards Guilsborough. The three fields were open, i.e. unhedged, and organised communally. Villagers had strips in each field which meant that their land was spread around the village but also meant that no one person got all the fertile land, and vice versa. The way to plough your strip was to start in the middle of it, at one end, run its length and then work clockwise around that out towards the edge. This saved lots of awkward turning but meant that the soil was always thrown up toward the centre of your land. This created the ridges and furrows still seen in many fields around the village today. The furrow so created became a natural drain and generally ran downhill. Every year one field would be left fallow and animals allowed to graze on it to manure it and restore fertility. These were common grazing rights, but animals were not welcome on cultivated fields. Field boundaries were grass ridges: hedges did not become the norm as boundaries until after enclosure in the late 18th Century.

Northamptonshire was part of the Parliamentary Enclosure boom in the 18th century, a relatively late date, and many examples of ridge and furrow remain locally around the village and in Watford. Some of the land around the village was marginal for arable use. When it no longer became economic to plough, it was easy to grass over and allow the drovers to use it to fatten their cattle on their way to market.

The Old Fire Station seems hopelessly inadequate to our eyes. We don't know when it was built but it was extended in 1876. It was obviously very important if your thatched cottage was on fire. You also needed to hope you were near a well, spring or pump! Generally speaking, fire stations were positioned near to the village church. A reverse peal of bells was rung to summon villagers to turn out and fight a fire. Individual houses carried their own insurance, and displayed a fire mark plaque above their front door as proof that they had paid up and were therefore entitled to be rescued.

Avenue House already mentioned is a most imposing building facing down Crown Lane. It was built for one of the Heygates, a doctor who worked in the area around 1750. Records of his practice survive in London. A serious fire in 1995 revealed that the house had thatch under the slate roof. This was sometimes for insulation, sometimes for modernisation. Other houses in the village took the cheaper option of using tin to cover the thatch. A third option was to use slate for the front of the house but tin for the rear, to keep up appearances. Mr. Crawley who kept the butchers shop at the top of Crown Lane, lived at Avenue House in the mid 20th century, with a slaughter house in Crown Lane. Mrs. Crawley, who died in January 2001, is remembered as a very well dressed woman.

Tower House is on the third side of this irregularly shaped triangle. Perhaps it was so named because of its imposing size. It has a hipped roof, with four arrises (angular side ridges) running up to a central ridge, rather than two gable ends and a central ridge. There are other examples of this in the village. Older villagers remember the house when it was owned by Entwistles, who took in apprentices for dressmaking. At one time Josie Hunt and then a Miss Hallett had a room in the house. Mrs Harriett Croxford learned dressmaking there as a girl. Mr Tom Payne owned it later on. If you look carefully at the boundary wall of this garden, you can see where the doors and windows of several cottages used to be. The wooden lintels remain, the gaps are blocked in by stone. In 1952 a report in the Daventry Express says that villagers were complaining that these cottages were unfit for habitation. The slaughter house in Crown Lane encouraged rats. Mr Payne demolished them in 1953 and villagers moved to the second phase of the Council houses in Guilsborough Road.

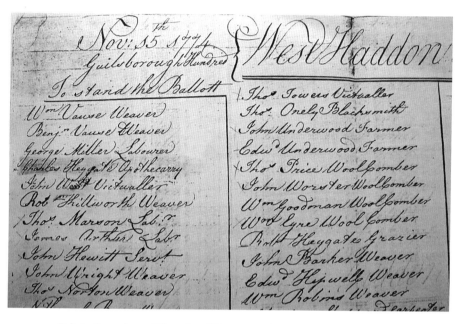

List showing Charles Heygate Apothecary in 1774.

The whole Crown Lane triangle may well be 'market infill', where the village's medieval marketplace was built over after it declined. We know that this market was going strong in 1292 because it was affecting the market in Northampton, and there was a petition by the town to move it from an unknown day to a Thursday to reduce the competition. It was still going but rather smaller as late as the 1720s. Triangular market places are very common and its position adjacent to the church is typical. The Crown may even have evolved from a market stall offering refreshments to buyers and sellers. The older name of the long arm of Crown Lane, known even today by older villagers as Chequers Lane, may be a reference to the market officials who would have been employed by Daventry Priory, the landlords, to collect market tolls and ensure fair dealing among traders. There is some evidence to suggest that the area began to be sold off for development around 1600.

Pytchley Court, developed around 1990, stands on the site of a builder's yard, which was owned by the Colbourne family. It runs off Crown Lane at right angles behind the Pytchley Hotel.

At the junction of these two lanes is Westfield Cottage. It was originally two cottages and stood in the grounds of Westfield house, now the Pytchley Hotel. Some of the staff for the house lived here. Mr Peach lived at the cottage nearest the church and was the chauffeur. Mr Wooding, the gardener/butler lived at the other. The cottages were knocked together by Ken Croxford's brother Bill in the 1950's.

Westfield Cottage.

Northampton Road

In this road is a development of council housing built in 1919, set well back from the road as it climbs steeply up the hillside, and still known as the 'New Houses'! The Festival Garden close by was named after the Festival of Britain in 1951. Previously, this was the site of old houses which were set very close to the road and made it very narrow. This shows up clearly on the 1900 Ordnance Survey map of the village. When the cottages were demolished, the road was deliberately widened to speed traffic which struggled up the steep escarpment on its way to Northampton.

The Festival Garden was once used by the village school for gardening but it was often a struggle as the ground was very stony. The land belongs to the Parish Council and one shilling was paid in rent. At one time there was a more serious horticultural business in the field behind. John Harding was a seedsman and nurseryman and established his business in 1878. Then it was taken over by Fred Ainge in 1912, on the site now occupied by the council houses, and no. 21 Northampton Road. His daughter, Hilda Stanley, still lives in the village. The West Haddon sign was placed in the Garden to mark the Millennium.

West Haddon Sign in the Festival garden.

The Banks leads off Northampton Road to the Playing Fields. There were originally two rows of cottages known as 'parish houses' owned by the parish and used to accommodate villagers unable to house themselves - a sort of forerunner of the council housing on Northampton Road. They were sold off to individuals in the 1870s and the remaining row was extensively rebuilt in 1975-6.

Guilsborough Road

The Post Office, a most important village asset, has been in this road as well as at 36 High Street. It used to be at number three Guilsborough Road, where a telephone box still stands outside the property. A post box stood outside number three until December 2000 when it was moved to be by the present Post Office in the High Street.

Numbers Three and Five Guilsborough Rd were once one building, a big house for its day. Westfield House (now the Pytchley) was probably built in its grounds. Number Five may be the oldest surviving house in the village with parts dating from 17th century. The return wall is of timber and lath above stone. On a summer walk around the village, Ken Croxford, who until recently lived there, pointed out that he had had to replace one of the timbers. Sure enough, it is slightly straighter than the rest. It may also have been a pub at one time, The Bell, which failed to survive the Temperance movement. Its situation, opposite the Baptist and now

Possibly the Oldest House in The Village.

demolished Wesleyan chapels, would not have helped. There are remnants of a forge behind the house.

Mr. Worcester, who recorded his occupation as 'gentleman', the first in the village to do so, lived here. One of the new roads off Morrison Park Road is named after this family. The last Miss Worcester died in 1941. She lived in Staffords Lane, moving finally to one of two cottages which stood next to the Graziers Arms further up the road out of the village. Villagers say she always wore a cloak. The History Group has recently been contacted by the Worcester family who are still going strong in New England, USA. Several of their ancestors were vicars, including the Rev William Worcester, whose forebears resided in West Haddon; he emigrated to New England in 1636. William Worcester was the village 'constable' and we have his report to the Hilary sessions in 1657.

Numbers 11 and 15 were also formerly one house - The Compass, another village pub. First records of it are from 1776, when it had a bread oven. You can see that it has been added to over the years. The top storey is (cheaper) brick, added when John West found that business was booming in guest houses in 1862. The deeds to the house talk about several messuages or tenements in 1858, but no map is included. Perhaps they were in the extensive grounds at the back. It was sold to Phipps brewery in 1888. The Home Guard used to meet here during the Second World War and stories from surviving members indicate it was every bit as chaotic as the much loved television series *Dad's army*. The Scouts also used it as headquarters for a time. By 1960, The Compass had been delicensed.

Further out of the village is the first side road - Elizabeth Road. The houses were originally built by the Council in 1953, Coronation Year, and named accordingly. The bungalows were built a little later. Some of them have hipped roofs echoing the style of the Pytchley and number 35 Guilsborough Road, Rokeby Cottage. The bungalows were built slightly later. Part of the house which used to stand at the entrance to Elizabeth Road, number 23 Guilsborough Rd, was demolished to give access to the land behind. Tailor Orland used to work there, and there was always a glass case outside showing his wares. The rest of number 23 was demolished in 1995 along with the remaining cob wall. The site has been developed as Eleanor Terrace, another royal name. Both Edward I and Henry II wives were called Eleanor.

The field at the end of Elizabeth Road was developed in the early 1990s for detached houses when Elizabeth Road itself had houses added to it and two further roads, Victoria Close and Church Close, were built. 'Close' originally meant a small, enclosed, usually hedged field to distinguish it from the extensive open fields in the pre-enclosure landscape. Victoria Close carried on the tradition of using the names of British female monarchs. and runs from Elizabeth Road towards All Saints Church. It was originally meant to be Church Close, but unfortunately, at the site meeting held to allocate the names, the map was held upside down, and Church Close is now the close furthest from the church! There

Victoria Close.

was a move to revert back to the original naming but the first houses in Church Close had been occupied by this time, and the residents were adamant that they would stick with the situation.

Back in Guilsborough Road is Rokeby Cottage, at number 35. It may have been a religious meeting house, part of the dissident movement in the village. It was a wheelwrights in the early 20th century, and later owned by Mr Mody, who had a business supplying varnish, polish and enamel. But why Rokeby? It could be a corruption of Rugby.

Further towards the outskirts of the village are two houses with a connected history. The furthest out, Redmoor House, boasts magnificent windows with stone mullions. Its name derives from Reedmoor probably because it was on the heathland between West Haddon and Guilsborough. There are still farmyard buildings just behind the house. It was the home of the Parnell family, who were very involved with enclosure in West Haddon. The other house, Parnells Barn, stood in the grounds of Redmoor House, literally as a barn until it was converted by Vic Wigley, about 1980. Morrison Park Road and Muncaster Close are built on land which used to belong to this farmhouse.

WEST HADDON
AND MEARS ASHBY, NORTHAMPTONSHIRE.

Particulars and Conditions of Sale of
A HIGHLY VALUABLE

FREEHOLD ESTATE,

COMPRISING A CAPITAL

STONE AND SLATED FARM HOUSE,

WITH CONVENIENT OUTBUILDINGS AND PREMISES, AND

91a. 2r. 32p.

Of very valuable Arable and Pasture Land, in about equal quantities, most eligibly situate in the Parish of West Haddon and having a very extensive frontage to the Guilsborough Road, and now in the occupation of Mrs. Elizabeth Parnell, as yearly Tenant thereof, and producing the Annual Rent of £230, and also

13a. 1r. 20p.

Of superior garden and accommodation Land, situate close to the village of Mears Ashby, and having extensive and valuable frontages, and now in the occupation of Mr. Thomas Sanders, as yearly Tenant thereof, and producing the Annual Rent of £34, which will be offered for Sale by Auction in several Lots by

Messrs. STAFFORD & ROGERS

AT THE

GEORGE HOTEL, NORTHAMPTON,

ON

SATURDAY, AUGUST 2ND, 1879,

AT THREE FOR FOUR O'CLOCK IN THE AFTERNOON.

The respective Tenants will on application show the Lots, and further particulars may be obtained from the Auctioneers, Bedford, and Chellington near Bedford, and of MR. PHILIP O. JERVIS,
SOLICITOR, UTTOXETER,
THE VENDORS' SOLICITOR.

J. R. PORTER, PRINTER, BEDFORD.

Estate Sale Notice.

Richard and Nathaniel Parnell were allocated 'allotments' at enclosure in 1765, as landowners rather than tenants. This meant they did well out of the change, with larger fields to cultivate all in one place, even though they were originally against the idea of enclosure. But the sale of the freehold estate in August 1879 names Mrs Elizabeth Parnell as yearly tenant, rather than owner. The land was arable and pasture and included a gravel pit.

Several Parnells are buried in the churchyard, including Richard in 1787, and his wife Elizabeth, in 1791.

In more modern times, Dick Parnell was a brain surgeon in Oxford and married his first cousin. His son, William, is remembered as a very tall upright man, who always wore handmade boots. When he died he was cremated and caused something of a sensation. How could such a big man fit in to such a small box?

Mr William Parnell, who bred poultry on a large scale, was Chairman of the Village Hall building committee. He bought the land in Guilsborough Road once occupied by the Wesleyan chapel, to turn it into a youth club. Eventually, however, the site was sold and the proceeds given to the Village Hall. His wife was secretary of the old Nursing Association. One particularly vicious storm in 1947 which took off the roofs of the two cottages in High Street, opposite the church, also flattened the Parnells' chicken huts and started a fire there by knocking over the incubators.

The first phase of the council houses in Guilsborough Road were built before the Second World War. The footings for the next phase provided a playground for children. The area was called 'The Concrete' by them. The rest were built in the early 1950s. The first families to move in reported that they were like palaces, within inside toilets. There was, however, no electricity and no running water in the first few weeks. The water tower had not been built, and water had to be drawn daily from Parnells at Redmoor farm or Atterburys at Manor Farm.

The Graziers public house, which, like The Crown, was once owned by Phipps, stood just before where the traffic 'shuttle' stands today. It was destroyed by fire. After a period of vacancy and dereliction it was being rebuilt and restored by Mann's brewery when it was again burnt down in 1979. After that the site was cleared and three detached houses were built there. The owner of number 42, the middle of the houses, has kept the name alive by calling it Grazier House. The name comes from the drovers who grazed their cattle on the pasture around the village to fatten them up before driving them on to market in Northampton and London.

Further down Guilsborough Road, an area of land known locally as Tom Patch's Brickyard- officially called The Old Brickyard - has being developed for detached houses of a larger size. The first recorded Tom Patch called himself a farmer although he only had a paddock attached to his cottage which he bought in 1729. He and his wife Elizabeth had six children but only one son, young Tom, survived. We know father Tom voted Tory in the 1748 General Election, as secret ballots were yet to come. He died suddenly in 1756. Son Tom, a shoemaker, married a village woman, Mary Spokes, in 1760. He was 32, she 33. They had a son, another Tom and a daughter. This Tom followed his father's trade, married Mary West in 1790 and their son William was born the following year. He was baptised on 27th November. His mother died a few days later on 4th December, and baby William on 9th. Tom, left on his own, discovered that his paddock yielded very good brick earth so he mortgaged the cottage and land to his brother-in-law, William West, a village tailor, and entered in to an agreement with a village builder, John Johnson.

The number of houses and therefore the population of the village has not always risen but waxed and waned (see the appendix). However, speculative building was possible at the beginning of 19th century when nationally the population was rising fast, possibly as a result of the end of the Napoleonic Wars with soldiers returning home. The Union canal was also completed at this time and the 'navvies' were no longer required. Between 1821 and 1827, Tom and his partner split his original cottage into three dwellings, converted a barn into another three and built seven more cottages. All this was on his original paddock-cum-brickyard. He died in 1838, aged 76. Records exist of a stone tablet, inset in one of the cottages, marked TP 1822, but its current whereabouts is unknown.

Vine Cottage, an old cottage with an imposing doorway and interesting window, stands further down the road towards the village. It was once the home and shop of the Ainge family, already mentioned in connection with horticulture, selling seeds. The shop window was where the sitting room is now. The counter stopped the door opening very far. Once a fat Weights and Measures man got stuck there when on an official visit.

The Wesleyan Chapel was built on the next plot of land, where today there is a bungalow which was lived in by Gladys Atterbury **(see page 42)** .The Chapel was built in 1810, set well back from the road. It was re-erected in 1847, renovated in 1886, but by the mid 1900's was semi-derelict. The dedication plaque for the chapel survives in a private collection.
'Wesleyan Cottage', now Manor Cottage, on the next plot at number 2, is a reminder.

The Baptist Chapel next door still stands and is going strong, part of the important non conformist tradition in the village.

Morrison Park Road, Muncaster Way, Lattimore, Parnell and Worcester Closes

At the moment, the last cul-de-sac at the edge of the village is Morrison Park Road, leading to Muncaster Way, both names connected with the story of public health in West Haddon. But the rapid growth West Haddon has experienced during the 1990s, and on into the 21st century, shows no sign of abating, so this may yet change. Further housing is being developed in Worcester, Parnell and Lattimore Closes at the time of writing.

Dr Morrison's memorial arch by the church has already been mentioned (See page 20). He bought a house, The Limes, now known as' Haddondale', in West End from Dr Stephenson. Dr Stephenson is fondly remembered but "no good for heart problems", as he was slightly deaf and couldn't use his stethoscope.

An Off Duty Photograph of Dr. Morrison.
Kindly donated by Dr. Daniels of Crick.

Dr Morrison was in the army at Tobruk. Although he owned a house and practised in the village he lived outside the village, in Elkington and Leicestershire for much of his life. He was an enthusiastic sportsman, famous in hunting circles for breeding a new type of beagle. A gentleman of substance, he had a painting by Canaletto hanging in his dining room, and one by Stubbs in his breakfast room. Experts would probably value the Canaletto more highly but he preferred the Stubbs. He was known for making house calls still dressed in his hunting pinks (as the red coats are known). The Morrison Cup, donated by him whilst still in practice, was competed for annually in the village carnival in the fifties. The carnival died out and was revived for a short time in the 1990s

The Yelvertoft & District Nursing Association was formed in 1932 with Mrs. Butler Henderson as President, and Mrs. W. Parnell as secretary/treasurer. The first nurse was Nurse Mayer followed by Nurse Muncaster.

Nurse Muncaster.

Nurse Muncaster was a native of Shropshire, a widow with a son and daughter when she came to Northamptonshire. She was first based in Winwick, at Bridge Cottage, where her house was often flooded out when the brook broke its banks. Enlisting the help of Mrs. Wykeham of Foxhill Manor, and other members of the nursing committee, she was found a new home in West Haddon at Dudley House, number one, on the corner of West End. It cost the committee £500 and she paid a nominal rent. Besides West Haddon, Nurse Muncaster covered the parishes of Winwick, Yelvertoft, Clay Coton, Lilbourne and Crick. She brought almost an entire generation of villagers into the world and their stories about her would fill a book on their own! Doctors were firmly pushed aside when she arrived at a confinement.

Arthur Vines, at one time the village milkman, recalls having to take her over the fields to Shenley Farm near Lilbourne, one night in March 1947, for a birth. There was very heavy snow that year, three or four feet deep and they had to go on his new Fordson tractor at one o'clock in the morning with Nurse Muncaster hanging on, standing on the step. All ended happily: the baby was born half an hour after they got there. The story was featured in the *Rugby Advertiser* as an extreme example of the problems suffered around the whole area at that time.

Nurse Muncaster was generally known to speak as she found and didn't suffer fools gladly. One patient fighting pneumonia in childhood recalled, "I knew I had to get better. She'd have killed me if I hadn't." Remember that there was no National Health Service until 1947, and local health arrangements were vital. She had the community very much at heart and organised square dances at The Crown to raise money for the new village hall.

Nurse Muncaster lived at Dudley House until 1982, when it became too large for her, and it was sold, the money being given to the Relief in Sickness Fund. She had bought a house for her sister, further along West End. Her sister having died, she moved in and lived there until her death in 1991, aged 96. There were other women too who acted as unofficial nurses having a 'natural feel' for healing including Nurse Grimshaw, Doris Webb's granny.

Dudley House had previously been the home of other notables, including Tailor Furniss, early in the 20th century. He would sit cross-legged in his window, plying his trade. The left hand window was the shop window and was made smaller when it became a home, Tailor Furniss moving to a smaller cottage in Station Road. During the Second World War, Jimmy Townsend, of Depper Townsend's family, was hit by an out of control Bren Carrier in the Second World War, which crushed him in to the brick wall on the corner near the house. There is still evidence of repair to the wall.

We have already thought about Parnell Close and Worcester Close. Lattimore Close is named after the man who was headmaster of West Haddon Primary School from 1936 to 1970. He was very active in village life, including being the Chief Air Raid Warden during World War Two. The main incident during this period was when a Lancaster and a Halifax bomber collided in mid air on the night of 5th and 6th December 1944. They were part of a bomber stream headed for a raid on Soest. The Lancaster's 4,000 pound bomb load exploded scattering debris over a wide area. The Halifax crashed in to the bank of the Grand Union canal at Yelvertoft wharf. There was only one survivor.

Mr Lattimore.

Atterbury Close, Field Close and Dairy Close

Off Guilsborough Road, on the opposite side of the road to Morrison Park Road is another group of streets, one of which is Atterbury Close. This is named after another prominent family in the village. The Atterburys are an old Northamptonshire family who came to West Haddon in 1848. They bought Manor Farm (where the road splits for Cold Ashby and Guilsborough), along with the Lordship of West Haddon. However the village has always been an 'open' village (unlike Watford for example) rather than a closed one entirely controlled by one person, which is probably why the village has grown faster than some of its neighbours.

Mrs Gladys Atterbury and Son Cllr Richard Atterbury.

The Atterburys sold Manor Farm at around the time of the Second World War, but remained - and remain - an important local family. Plaques to several members are erected in the Parish Church, and the was porch restored by the family and friends of Harry Atterbury, who lived from 1907 to 1981, partly in the village but also at Sharley Cop in Ravensthorpe. Gladys Atterbury, his wife, was active in local politics as a member both of Daventry District Council and, for 45 years, of West Haddon Parish Council. She served as West Haddon chairman for three of those years and as leader of Daventry Council in 1977/78. Mrs. Atterbury died in 1998, a greatly respected local resident. Her son Richard, who lives at Crick, continues the tradition as a district councillor.

Atterbury Close, along with Field Close, was developed in the early 1960s. Field Close, when it was still a field, had the village duck pond in it. More housing was added at the end of the road in the late 1980s with a cul-de-sac created in the field known as Dairy Close. The road bears this name. The adjacent field is Home Close, still open land. Cattle were brought to these fields at night for safety. There were traces of ridge and furrow ploughing here, a reminder of the feudal agricultural system. One patch here was not ploughed but left flat, and the hay ricks which provided winter feed for the cattle were built on it.

Old Forge Drive

Old Forge Drive almost tells its own story. A village forge existed at the entrance to the land on which the road is built. Martin Booker lived here until 1989 although it had ceased to function as a forge by then. His grandfather Charlie ran it about 80 years ago, with his son, also Charles, following him into the business. Charlie's niece, Dolly, used to watch him pumping the bellows which stood by the glowing fire. She remembered him letting her and other onlookers have a go. The horseshoe was heated until red hot and then applied to the horse's foot where it stuck with the aid of nails. A number of well off village people hunted, as well as using horses for transport. These included Colonel Welman who lived at what is now the Pytchley, Dr. Stephenson, the Heygates at the top of Crown Lane, Mr. Parnell from Guilsborough Road and Captain Fitzroy from Foxhill. People from outlying villages also came to Mr. Booker. Captain Gordon had an estate in Wiltshire, but used Oak House in West End as his hunting lodge.

The Old Forge.

Behind the forge was a wheelwrights and wagon repair shop. When the forge was being demolished in 1989, an interesting construction was revealed. The ground floor was cob, probably quite old. Cob was made from mud and cow dung which was a fire retardant. Animal hair (possibly from cows) was added in to strengthen the mix and could still be identified as the wall was demolished. There is still a cob wall at number 12 Guilsborough Road and at other sites around the village. The equipment in the forge mainly went to the County Museum, but the Local History Group still has the bellows.

Westburys who developed the site have christened some of the houses in keeping with this name eg Anvil Cottage and Horseshoe Cottage. The rest of the site was field.

West End

This is another 'end', which, as we have seen, means a new extension of an old village. Thus West End was a new part of West Haddon, with houses being built out from the centre, presumably reaching out towards the direction in which trade came in to the village on the main road. Like 'South End' the name West End was originally an informal one, as addresses were given as 'Dunchurch Road', reflecting the main road's importance. At the end of the 13th century, the fast rising population encouraged the Lord of the Manor, Daventry Priory, to build housing to rent out and increase their income. Perhaps West End was started before South End, and was finished before the Black Death wiped out a large percentage of the population, around 1349. There are rumours of mass burials made at this time, in the form of a large grave in front of the main door of the church when the new footpath was built in the 1950's.

Nearby Elkington was a thriving village before the Black Death but never recovered. There were repeated visitations of the plague and it took a long time for the population to increase. It was probably not until the 17th century that more new houses were needed. You have to remember, too, that each parish was financially responsible for its poor people which included providing them with housing. One way to reduce this burden was to refuse to build houses and thus force 'down and outs' away.

The Sheaf is one of the oldest pubs in the village. The Newman family were brewing there in 1581. It is on record that they broke the licensing laws of the time. An energetic local historian in the 19th century discovered that there was a skeleton in the cellars. This was said to be the remains of Boudicca (Boadicea), who retreated there to die of wounds after fighting the Romans! (History says she died of poison). It has been owned by a number of breweries, including Hunt Edmonds, reckoned by connoisseurs in the village to be one of the best beers. There was a fish and chip shop down here, behind and to the right of The Sheaf just after the Second World War.

There is an interesting little 'backwater' further along from The Sheaf, but before The Green. It consists of an L shape of two rows of cottages starting at right angles to the main road. The building parallel to the main road, once known as Mount Pleasant, or Shepherd's (or Sheppards) Mount, is two homes now, but was once three. The other houses are at right angles to these, Shepherd's Row. Nurse Muncaster lived out her retirement at number 27. It is officially numbered as part of West End. The local names may indicate some further connection with Daventry Priory.

This area may also have been the scene of the Great Fire of West Haddon, since there are no old properties, and near The Sheaf is a truncated barn with charred timbers at one end. Fire was a terrible hazard in a time when buildings generally had highly flammable thatched roofs, floors were covered in rushes and lighting was by candle. We know the Fire happened in 1657: its actual location is unknown but 18 bays (window's widths) of houses were destroyed. Such was the scale of the disaster that a surviving barn had to be converted into a house for the survivors, who were officially allowed to beg for alms.

The Green, where the Village Hall and school stand, is an integral part of our village, as with many villages in the southern part of the country. It was once larger and completely covered in grass, and has changed much over the years. There were two thatched cottages here on the site of the village hall. Villagers remember there being laurel bushes as well. The cottages were fairly poor, having no electricity when the rest of the village had been connected to mains supply.

The Old School Master's House.

The Reading Room was here, replaced by the Village Institute, built 1903. The latter is fondly remembered by villagers as the place that fruit canning used to take place during World War Two. Special hand operated machines were needed for this. A new Village Hall then replaced this building in 1958.

The school has progressively expanded to accommodate growing numbers of village children - a schoolmaster's house was demolished in 1970 to make room for enlargement.

It is believed that one of the village's leading medieval public houses, the Red Lion, stood at the entrance to the Green, Tudor Cottage. It is the only remaining part of a much larger building. The part which used to jut out into West End was demolished to ease road congestion. This public house was the meeting place of the Turnpike trustees and therefore an important place in the village. Mr Lattimore always told the school children to cross West End here as it was the narrowest point. However it was still possible to play football in the street here before the Second World War.

On the other side of West End, just past the current vicarage, there used to be another forge, part of the Townley family business, the property being shown as 'The Park' in the 1800 deeds. Besides the smithy, there was a wagon repair shop, a coffin making business, and a gas making plant. He is also credited with inventing the Townley Ram. The one in West Haddon used a reservoir at the top of the 'rec', from where water was fed by gravity down to the churchyard by the Crown Lane gate, to the Hall, and other large houses. It was popular with the well to do and the inventor was pleased to advertise his extensive list of clients. To demonstrate the effectiveness of his ram, he erected some pipes in trees at the back of his site, pumping water up to the top. A cascade descended from about 100 feet up, a most effective piece of marketing! There are still one or two rams in use today. Chappie Townley's story is told in 'Milestones and Memories' This is where the Lord family, descendants of the Townleys, lived until towards the end of the 20th century. They turned the forge into a delightful flower shop. When the Lord family sold up, three properties were established here. The house furthest from West End is Townley Barn.

Just further along is Oak House, number 10, one of the oldest houses in the village. Edward Kirtland lived in the house where Hopwells antiques is now, in the High Street, but moved out in favour of his son and daughter-in-law when he remarried. He brought his new wife to this magnificent house which was then 'on the edge of town', and marked the occasion with a plaque EEK 1689.The house had a ballroom at one time and you can tell by looking at it that further various alterations have been made. The latest was probably around 1820. It was also the hunting lodge where Captain Gordon stayed. It has also been used as a school room for the village school. Navvies working on the construction of the M1, which opened as far as Crick in 1959, were accommodated at Oak House.

The cottages further along are much higher than the road but we don't know why. The road is very narrow here even though it was part of turnpike. It must have been developed before 1720. One cottage, The Shambles, was a butcher's shop selling locally raised beef of high quality, properly hung. There was a small slaughterhouse behind it at one time owned by the Judkins family. Ralph Judkins still lives on a farm on the edge of the village.

Rupert Cottage is nearby. Nowadays, it boasts a plaque to Rupert bear but perhaps the connection is with Prince Rupert and the Battle of Naseby?

Slyes Close is on the edge of the village. Nine houses were built in 1971-72, on land previously owned by Philip Wykeham of Rush House, at the junction of West End, Crick Road and Yelvertoft Road. The Close is named after William Walter Slye who is believed to have built Rush House. The date stone on the Market Field footpath behind the house is for 1887. The Slye family were another medical dynasty in West Haddon, and were related by marriage to the Heygate family. There is a memorial window in All Saints Church to Thomas Walter Slye MRCS and his wife Elizabeth and also to Charles John Slye and his wife Ann. William Walter Slye who was John's brother erected this in 1879. William Walter also has a window, dated 1906, commissioned by Fanny Nunns, his housekeeper. They are buried side by side in the churchyard. William Walter is listed as having loaned money to build the schoolmaster's house.

Behind Rush House is Market Field. The forebears of villagers spoke of "coming to market": the cattle market held here, mentioned in the sale of Redmoor House in 1879, were organised by the Underwood family at one time. The Northampton *Mercury and Echo* for March 1878 has an item about a new market starting up and proving very successful. It doesn't record who ran it.

The row of buildings opposite Slyes Close is The Almshouses. They were built by William Lovett in 1846 and endowed in 1857, being maintained from the rent from the Charity Fields on the western outskirts of the village. There is a plaque to 'William Lovett of West Haddon Grange' in the church. He died in 1859 aged 78 and is buried in the churchyard next to his parents. His sister, Mrs. Catherine Woodcock, paid £50 for the clock, known as 'Chloe', atop the almshouses. The clock was refurbished in the 1990s.

The Village Almshouses.

Outlying properties

Field and farm names also give us clues as to their history. The field names around West Haddon tell a whole story by themselves. On the road to Northampton is Ryehills Farm, and the field map of 1932 shows us the adjacent areas of First Rye Hills and Second Rye Hills. This was the eastern rye area. Rye was an important part of the agricultural system of the Middle Ages and would grow on poor land. A western area for rye is thought to have been located where Windmill Hill is today at the top of the gated road to Winwick. We know there was a windmill there in 1765 as it was mentioned in the Enclosure Act. As well as the windmill on the road to Northampton near Torkington Farm, there was also a water mill in Mill Meadow, adjacent to the Long Buckby boundary by Foxhill Road.

On Watford Road, right on the Parish boundary, is Washbrooke farm. Here at last is a handy stream for use by the villagers. The sheep, as the name implies, were brought down here for washing prior to being sheared. There was also a sheep dip just off Guilsborough Road, near where the doctor's surgery now stands in Muncaster Way.

Glebe Farm, on Winwick Road, shows that this was built on church or glebe land. Wold Farm, on Crick Road, means that the farmland was carved out of scrub or woodland. The nearby Grange Farm, also known as West Haddon Grange, was owned by William Lovett, benefactor of The Almshouses. It was bought by the Litchfield family in 1920 from the Church Commissioners. Charles Litchfield is noted as the main landowner in West Haddon at that time and the family is still going strong. Lily Holroyd, nee Litchfield, lived across the road at Little Coppits (a corruption of Little Coppice?) until her death in 1998.

There are many other family names with a long association with the village, yet to be commemorated. The research into all the people involved evokes a richly detailed history of the village, in which villagers took an active part as members of their community. Then, as now, there were 'characters' who made life so much more interesting.

Human nature often protests at being just a 'number', especially in an increasingly computerised world. We feel the need to retain personal identity. We may or may not be able to influence the name of a road or development, but we can certainly give our 'castle' an identity if we wish. We can also hand on to future generations clues about the past through these names.

The village of West Haddon has developed over many years, and is a fascinating mix of old and new. Traffic rushes along our tarmac roads today, often following the same route established several hundred years ago, yet it was only in 1910, to mark the accession of George V, that cobbles started to give way to slate as paving material. This was done piecemeal as house owners were expected to contribute towards the piece of road outside their house.

We are part of a continuing development and the pace of change is getting faster. The A14 trunk road opened in the early 1990s. Work on DIRFT, the rail freight terminal at Crick began in the same decade. These influenced our village in some way and will continue to do so. We wait to see if the village bypass will go ahead.

Not everything is known about the roads and houses mentioned. West Haddon Local History Group would be delighted to hear from you if you can add to, or indeed amend, anything written here.

Appendix

The Population of West Haddon.

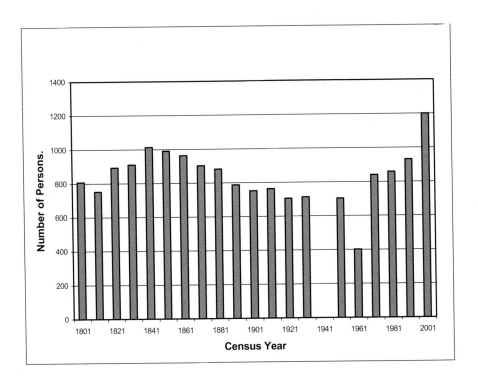

The number of persons shown for the year 2001 is an approximation.

It should be noted that a census was not taken in 1941 during the 2nd world war.